More
Little Ways
to Praise

Written and Illustrated by
Kathy Arbuckle

BARBOUR
PUBLISHING, INC.

Member of the
Evangelical Christian
Publishers Association

Published by Barbour Publishing, Inc.
        P.O. Box 719
        Uhrichsville, Ohio 44683
        http://www.barbourbooks.com

Printed in China.

Thy Word is a lamp unto my feet, and a light unto my path.

Psalm 119:105

For Cousins

Michael Joseph,
Meghan Brooks,
&
Erin Martha

Bible Praises for Preschoolers

For God is the King of all the earth: sing ye praises with understanding.

Psalm 47:7

All the nations of the world have leaders or kings. Some of these leaders are very powerful and rule over large, wealthy countries of many people. But even if you took all of the leaders and their money and power and put them all together, they would not be anywhere close to being as great as God. God rules over the whole earth. He is so mighty that He reigns over the entire universe! Nothing happens without God knowing about it and letting it happen. Give great praise to the mighty Lord.

What can you praise God for today? 9

to God

Whoso offereth praise glorifieth me...

Psalm 50:23

When you tell God how great He is you are praising Him. When you thank Him for all that He does for you and others you are praising Him, too. You can praise the Lord by talking to Him or praying, by singing songs to Him, even by drawing a picture for Him. He hears and sees all of your praises and He is pleased. Praise honors and glorifies God. It shows how important He is to you and how much you love Him.

What can you praise God for today?

Bible Praises for Preschoolers

In God I will praise his word, in God I have put my trust...

Psalm 56:4

God has given us His special book, the Bible, to teach us what is right. Even though the Bible was written so many, many years ago, it still teaches us today. God speaks to His people through the words He has written and shows us how to live and serve Him. The more you know about the Bible the more you know about God. You learn that you can trust Him to do what is best for you because He loves you so much. For that you should praise Him.

Bible Praises for Preschoolers

Make a joyful noise unto God, all ye lands...

Psalm 66:1

What noises sound happy to you? Maybe people laughing, singing, clapping their hands and making music? All over the world people know how to make sounds of joy. When you think about how special God is and about His kindness and love, it makes you happy. He gives you so many reasons to celebrate and rejoice. So sing and laugh. Clap your hands and make music. Your joyful praise will reach up to heaven and please God's ears.

What can you praise God for today? 15

Bible Praises for Preschoolers

Blessed be the Lord, who daily loadeth us with benefits, even the God of our salvation.

Psalm 68:19

Think of the things God does for you every day. He makes the sun come up in the morning to brighten the world. He gives you love and takes care of you. God gives you good food to eat and clothes to wear. You may even have friends and toys to play with today. God gives you so much each day and often He gives you more than you need. He also gave His only Son Jesus to save you. Praise God for giving such precious gifts of love.

What can you praise God for today? 17

Bible Praises for Preschoolers

Let the heaven and earth praise him, the seas, and every thing that moveth therein.

Psalm 69:34

God is so amazing that all of His creation praises Him. All of the clouds, stars, the sun and moon, and the birds that fly in the sky praise God. If the rocks and mountains could speak, you would hear them praising the Creator, too. All of the animals that walk, run, hop, crawl, or slither on the ground give honor to the Lord. Even the waves on the sea leap with joy as they rejoice in praise. Join with all creation and praise the Lord!

What can you praise God for today? 19

Bible Praises for Preschoolers

But I will hope continually, and will yet praise thee more and more.

Psalm 71:14

Sometimes a problem can seem so big that you don't know how to solve it. No matter how big that problem is, it can never be bigger than God. You must remember to ask God for help when things look bad. You can always have hope because God is always with you to protect you and be your best friend. Best friends always care about each other.

What can you praise God for today? 21

Bible Praises for Preschoolers

For thou, Lord, art good, and ready to forgive; and plenteous in mercy unto all them that call upon thee.

Psalm 86:5

When you do a bad thing it makes God sad. It can also hurt the people around you. Even though your sin displeases God, He will forgive you and forget the sin if you tell Him you are very sorry and will try to never do that bad thing ever again. God is so good that He has lots of forgiveness to give to everyone who asks for it from their hearts. Praise our Holy God Who loves us enough to forgive us.

What can you praise God for today?

The Lord on high is mightier than the noise of many waters, yea, than the mighty waves of the sea.

Psalm 93:4

Have you ever been on a boat? Maybe you went out on a lake or river or even on the ocean. Did you see the waves? In a storm the waves on the water can grow to be very big because of the strong wind. They roar as they toss and crash, spraying water everywhere. There is a lot of power in the waves. God made all of the lakes, rivers, and seas and rules over them. There is no one mightier anywhere. His love for you is as strong as He is.

What can you praise God for today?

Bible Praises for Preschoolers

Enter into his gates with thanks-giving, and into his courts with praise: be thankful unto him, and bless his name.

Psalm 100:4

Do you celebrate Thanksgiving Day? Maybe you share a turkey dinner and enjoy some pumpkin pie for dessert with your family. Thanksgiving Day is a special day when we thank God for all He has given to us. But we should be thankful every day! After all, the Lord takes good care of us each and every day. Tell God "Thank you" in your praises and prayers every day of the year.

What can you praise God for today?

From the rising of the sun unto the going down of the same the Lord's name is to be praised.

Psalm 113:3

Does God do good things for only part of the day? Does He go away on vacation or take time off from His work? No. He is busy loving you and caring for you all of the time. You are so special and important to Him that He is always watching over you. What a good thing it is to be loved so much by God. All through the day, from sunrise to sunset, think about God and give Him praise.

What can you praise God for today?

Bible Praises for Preschoolers

I love the LORD, because he hath heard my voice and my supplications.

Psalm 116:1

Are you a good listener? Can you sit quietly while someone speaks to you? God is the greatest listener. He is able to hear everyone's prayers at the same time and answer those prayers when and how He knows it is best. God is never too busy to hear you. Even if you only have a little prayer about the smallest thing, He hears you. You can talk to God one hundred times a day and He will listen to every single word. He will always hear your praises, too.

What can you praise God for today? 31

Bible Praises for Preschoolers

I will bless the LORD at all times: his praise shall continually be in my mouth.

Psalm 34:1

When is the best time to praise God? In the morning? At dinner time? When it is night? You should praise God all of the time! God never sleeps. All the day long He watches over you, protecting you, teaching you, loving you. Even when you are asleep at night He is right there covering you with His goodness and love, like a blanket. So, as you go through your day, remember to praise God every time you think of Him. After all, He never forgets about you.

What can you praise God for today?   33

Bible Praises for Preschoolers

O taste and see that the LORD is good: blessed is the man that trusteth in him.

Psalm 34:8

Do you like ice cream, apple pie, or chocolate? All of these things taste so good. We like them so much that we come back for more! That is how God is. He is so good that you will always want to be near Him. Time with God is the most important part of your day. So talk to Him and give Him praise. You will be so happy knowing that your good and great Heavenly Father is taking perfect care of you.

What can you praise God for today? 35

Bible Praises for Preschoolers

Thy mercy, O LORD, is in the heavens; and thy faithfulness reacheth unto the clouds.

Psalm 36:5

Have you ever watched the clouds float way overhead in the sky? It's fun to find ones shaped like animals or castles or even people. Clouds are up very high in the air. God's faithfulness is as high as the clouds. He keeps every single promise He ever makes. He is also merciful, which means He doesn't always punish those who deserve to be punished. God's faithfulness and mercy reach all the way up to the clouds and even higher! Let your praise be heard up to the sky, too.

What can you praise God for today?   37

Bible Praises for Preschoolers

How excellent is thy lovingkindness, O God! Therefore, the children of men put their trust under the shadow of thy wings.

Psalm 36:7

When baby chickens hatch from eggs they are very small and need to be cared for. Their mother watches over them and teaches them how to find food so they can grow. Sometimes there is danger nearby and the mother hen gathers her babies under her wings to protect them. She will even shelter them beneath her wings at night to keep them warm and dry. God protects you like that. He keeps you safe under His wings of lovingkindness.

What can you praise God for today?   39

Bible Praises for Preschoolers

Many, O LORD my God, are thy wonderful works which thou hast done, and thy thoughts which are to usward...

Psalm 40:5

Did you know God thinks about you? King David said God has more thoughts about you than there are grains of sand. Just think about all the beaches, deserts, and streambeds there are in the world and how many tiny grains of sand there must be. That is a lot of sand grains and a lot of thoughts God has for you. You are special to God, so special that He wants to do wonderful things for you. Let your thoughts today be filled with praises for God.

What can you praise God for today?   41

Bible Praises for Preschoolers

Let all those that seek thee rejoice and be glad in thee: let such as love thy salvation say continually, The LORD be magnified.

Psalm 40:16

Many stories are about people looking for treasure. Why do they search for jewels and gold? Because the treasure is valuable and worth a lot. God's love for you is priceless. But God gives His love as a free gift to those who want to be close to Him. He should be the most important thing in your life. You will want to tell everyone about Him and show them His love. Just like a magnifying glass makes things easier to see, you can make God's love easier for others to see, too.

What can you praise God for today?

Bible Praises for Preschoolers

As the hart panteth after the water brooks, so panteth my soul after thee, O God.

Psalm 42:1

Deer are wild animals that live in the woods and meadows. Sometimes a deer can become very thirsty. He will search hard and walk a long way up and down hills and mountains until he finds a cool, clear stream to drink from. God is so good that you should be like that deer, only you are seeking after God, not water. If you are close to God, you can easily "drink" the love He has for you.

What can you praise God for today?   45

Bible Praises for Preschoolers

Hope thou in God: for I shall yet praise him, who is the health of my countenance, and my God.

Psalm 42:11b

To hope is to expect something good. The Bible tells us to put our hope in God. That means you should trust God to always take perfect care of you. He knows better than anyone else what is good for you. Your family, all of the things you have, the food you eat every day, even your health—all of these good things come from God. Praise Him for what He has done for you and also for the good things He will do for you in the future.

What can you praise God for today?

Let every thing that hath breath
praise the LORD. Praise ye the LORD.

Psalm 150:6